The Calamity of Desire

By

R. C. Webb

Black Cat Publishing

Dark Home of the New Surrealism

San Miguel de Allende, Mexico

The Calamity of Desire

The Calamity of Desire

Is not always what it seems…

But the outcome, tragically

Is always the same

3-Ring Tsunami

80-100 foot seas

Perilously to windward

The Cosmic Calamity

The Tenets of Desire

Greater than the sea

An audience of pale humans

Make a joke of Reality

Polly Morph and Molly Gwain-YA

And Dog Butt Ugly too

Surrender to the Surrealist notion

That none of this may be true

But, to seriously ingenious phrophets…

Breeders of the Cosmic Ruse

The outcome is still the same:

With the joke still on You

Boo Hoo

And unfortunately enough, the Joke is on me too!

The Calamity of Desire

Vol 1: Requiem to the Perfect Storm
O Lord of the Fathoms
Hear our plea
For those in peril
On the Sea

Requiem for the Andrea Gail
Lost off the Flemish Cap Oct. 1991 in what became known as:
The Perfect Storm
With all hands lost

The Calamity of Desire

Behold! The High-butted Polly Morph

Her Anthropomorphic flare adds to her charms

The windows of the Heavens foreclose on the danger

The Tsunami below means only harm

"MAY DAY! MAY DAY!"

No Gods will answer

At least not an Anthropomorphos known

To the Perfect Storm, full fisted and cruel

The Calamity of Desire is due to unfold

Real heads and strong arms

are inherently human

When attached to a mortal's

corporeal frame

Guiding lost souls

into the crevasse of tomorrow

Far past the grey marble

where one still needs a name

On the edge of tomorrow,

The Black Hole is immortal

No beginning and no end

can it give or receive

Dead or alive there is no difference

"Creation = Destruction"

will enlighten or deceive

Polly Morph got the

"MAY DAY" running

But for sex she ignored

the wreckage far below

The oil lamps of the Gods

illuminate the disaster

Sirens wail and Oracles

weep to and fro

What restrains the

mortal's soul in flight

The passing from

Man to Spirit in vain

Spirit or Man trapped

in the flotsam

And jetsam

where no mortal

can remain

Polly Morph was once

a gung-Ho Sea Ranger

Her side-kick Molly Gwain-YA was too…

Scanning the "MAY DAY"

for earthly remains

Survival suits orange

with mortals turned blue

"Only drowning men can see her…"

Our Lady of the Harbor

Leonard Cohen was dead serious as the dead

"All men shall be sailors,

until the Sea shall set free them…"

Those of us who have seen it

know it is not "in your Head"

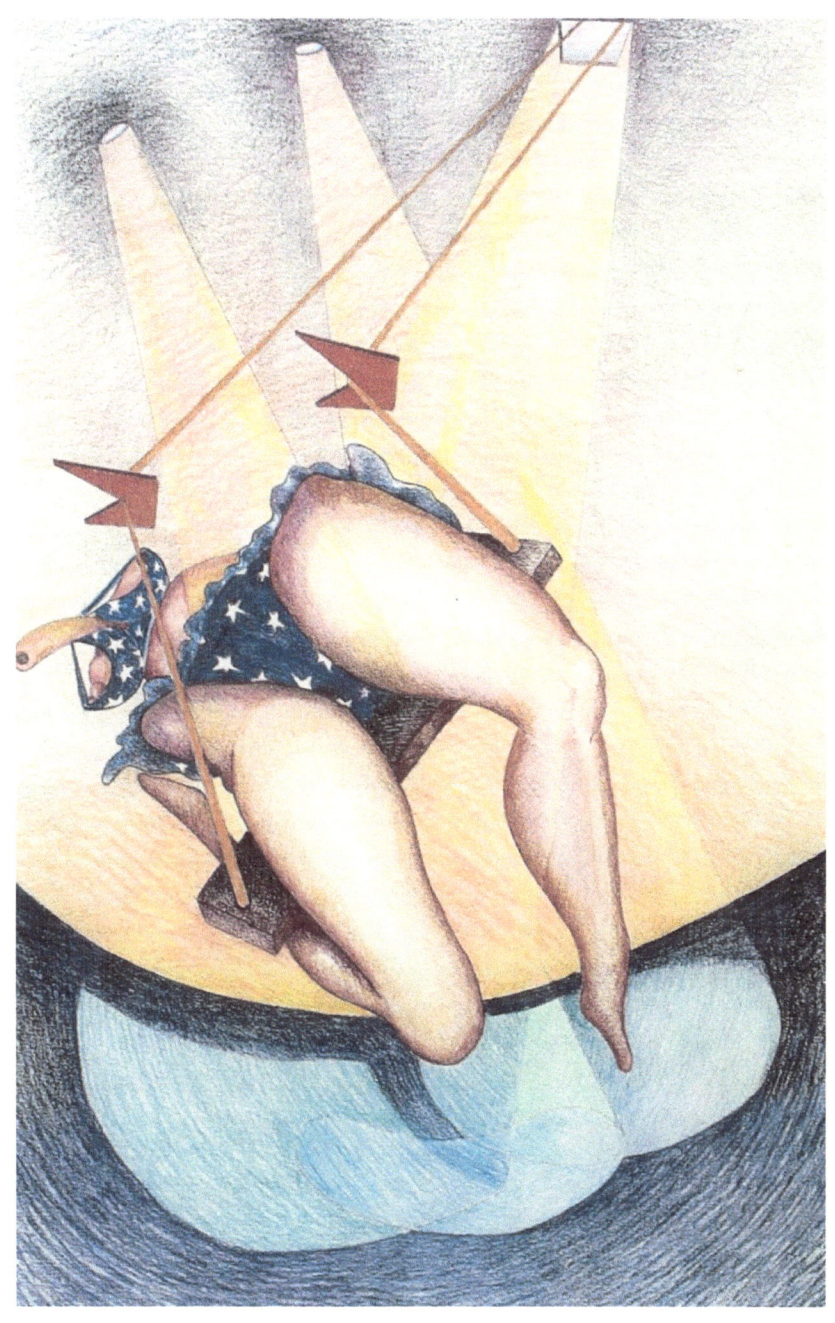

In the Cosmic Cirque de Corporeal, Polly Morph
Tends to the Sea, Our Guardian spots
The fleeting Souls down Below

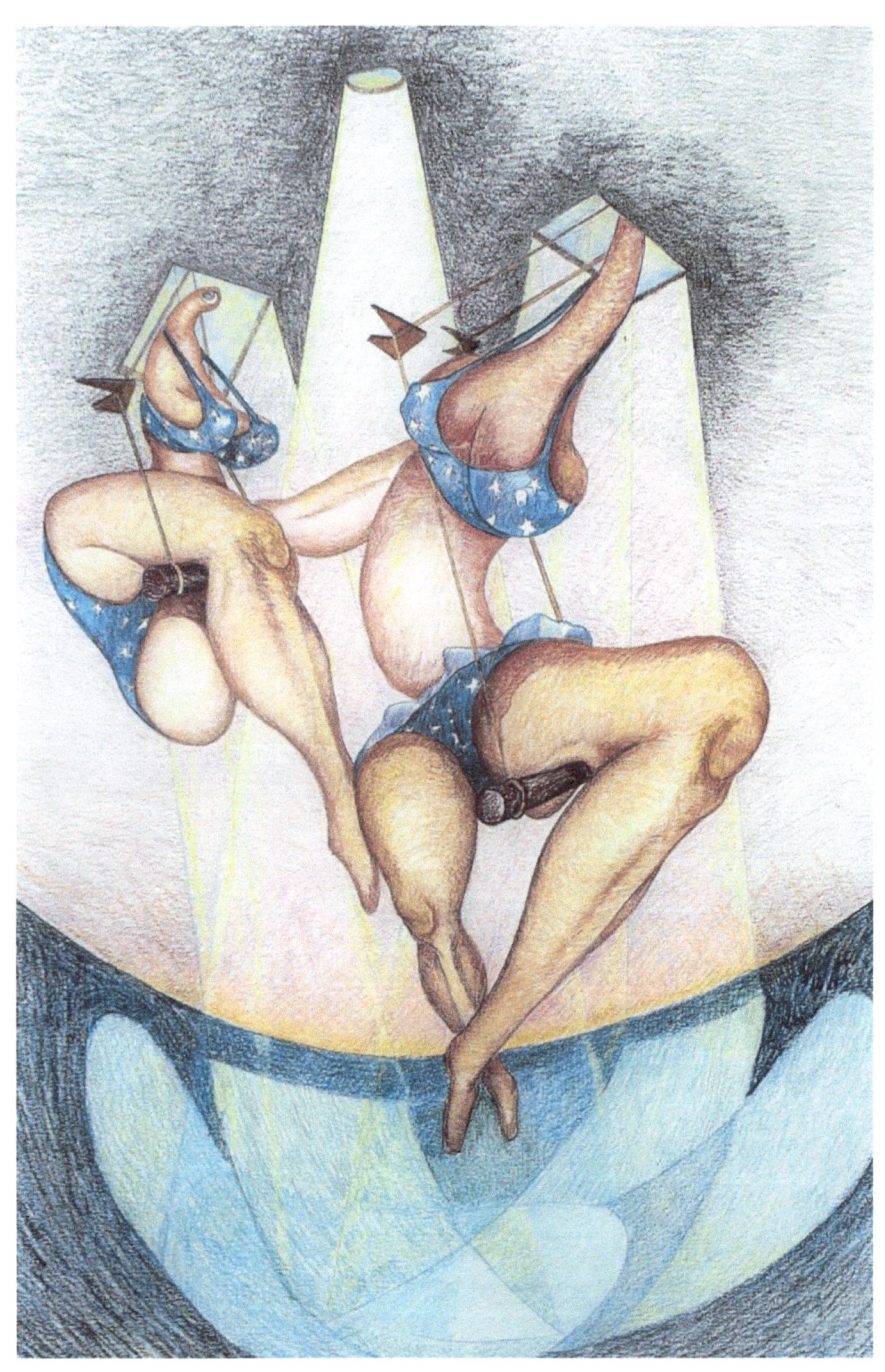

Across the vortex, the Anthropomorphos emerge
But without fresh souls they can't get back in
Morph God is compassionate, but not thinned skin

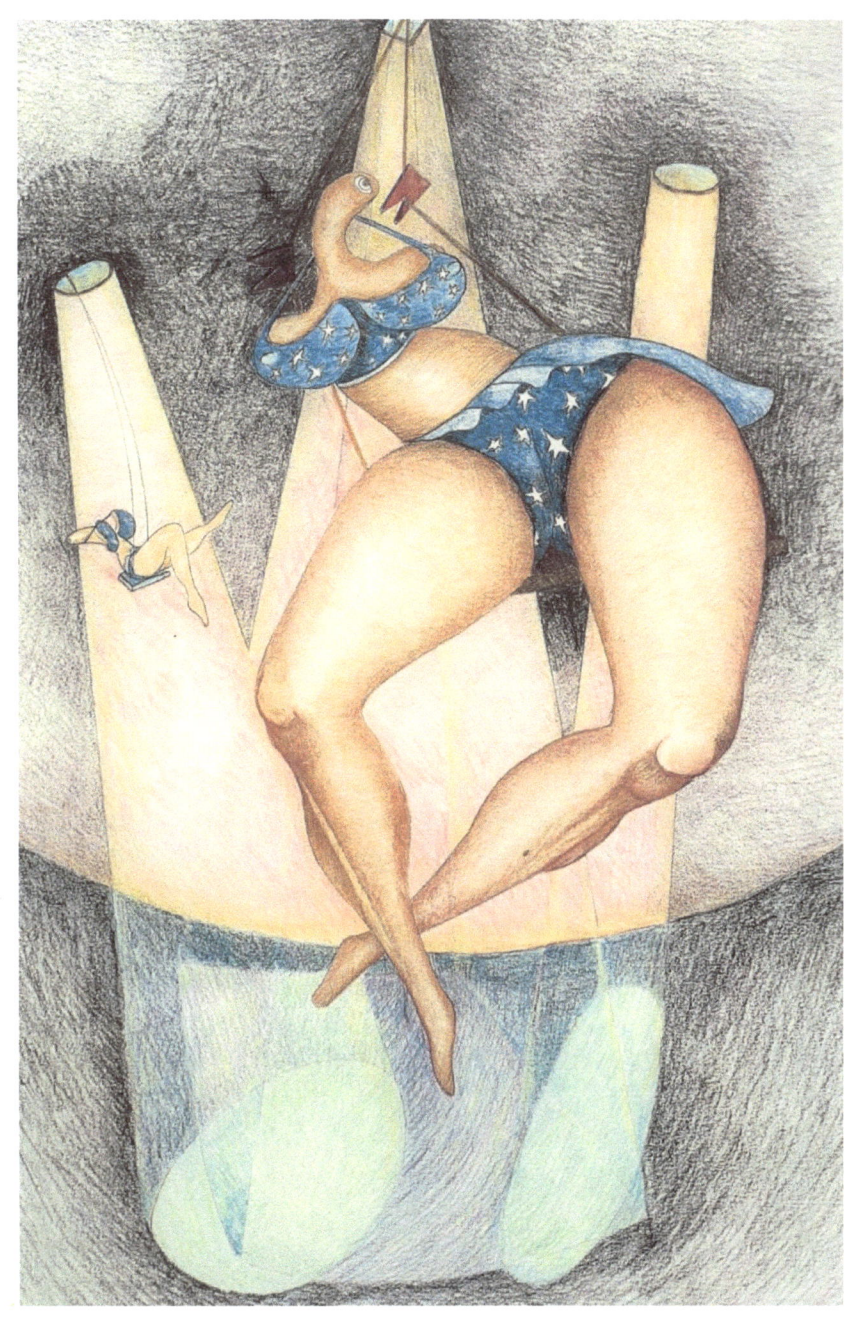

An armlessly beautiful botched transgender
Morph God sends backup Sea Ranger Molly Gwain-YA
Gung-Ho Anthropomorphos to the Rescue!

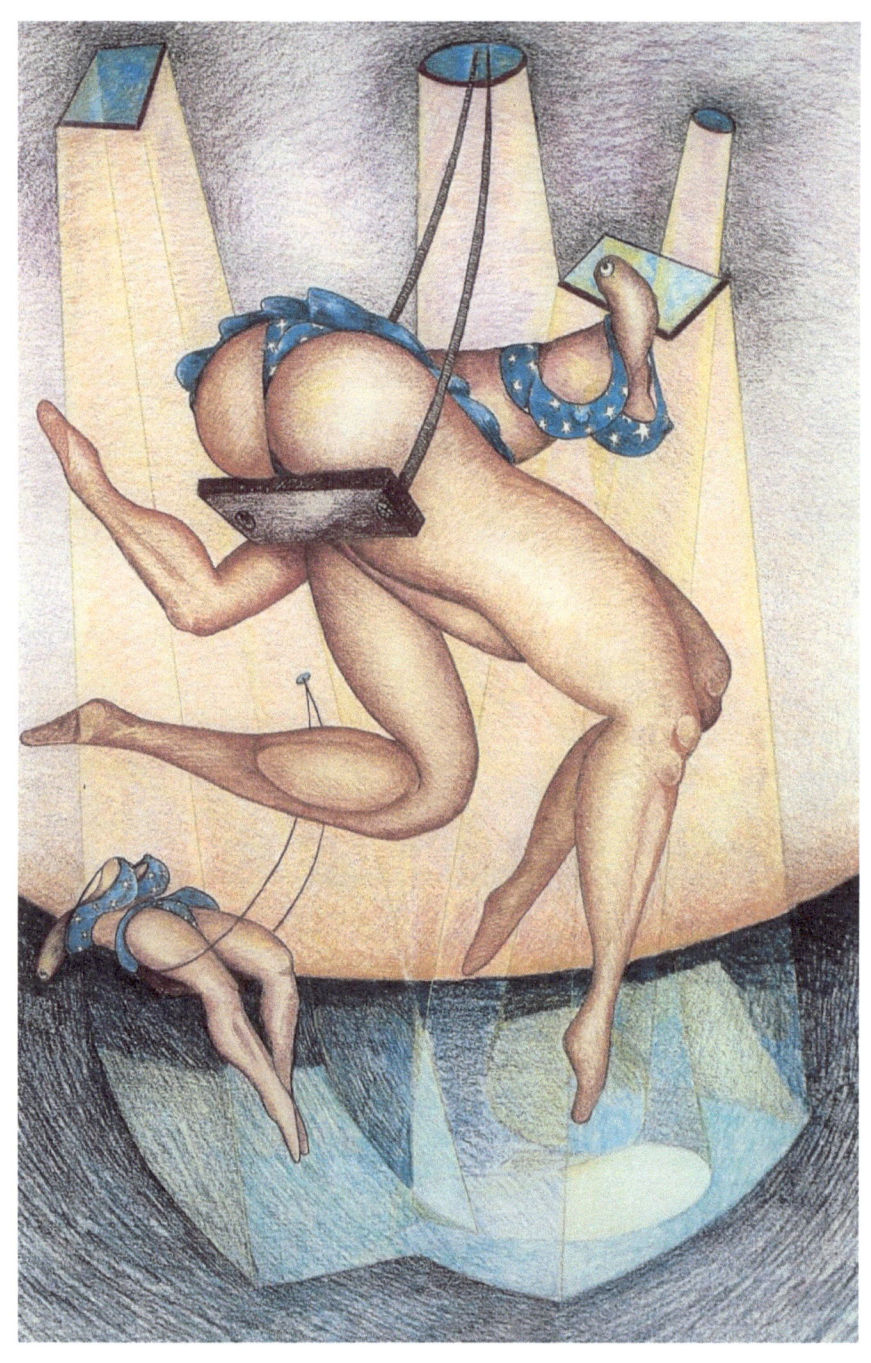

Polly Morph, humanly aroused, swings into action unreal
Sprouting two more legs and a "U Know What"
Back-up Booty for her next big move!

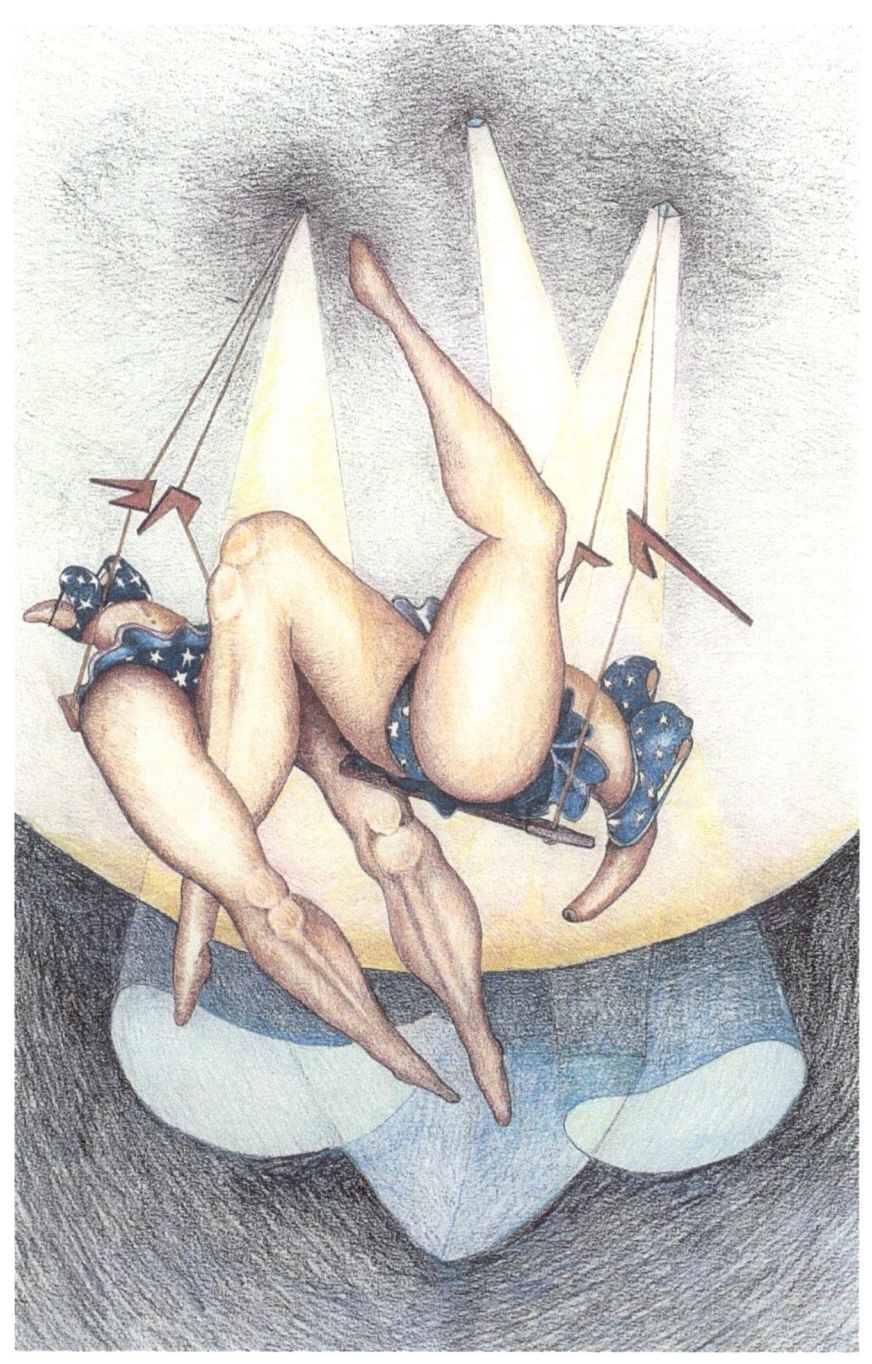

Using a radical leglock maneuver, Polly Morph cops Molly
In time for the show—just not the one down below
Lost souls go forsaken into the dark unknown

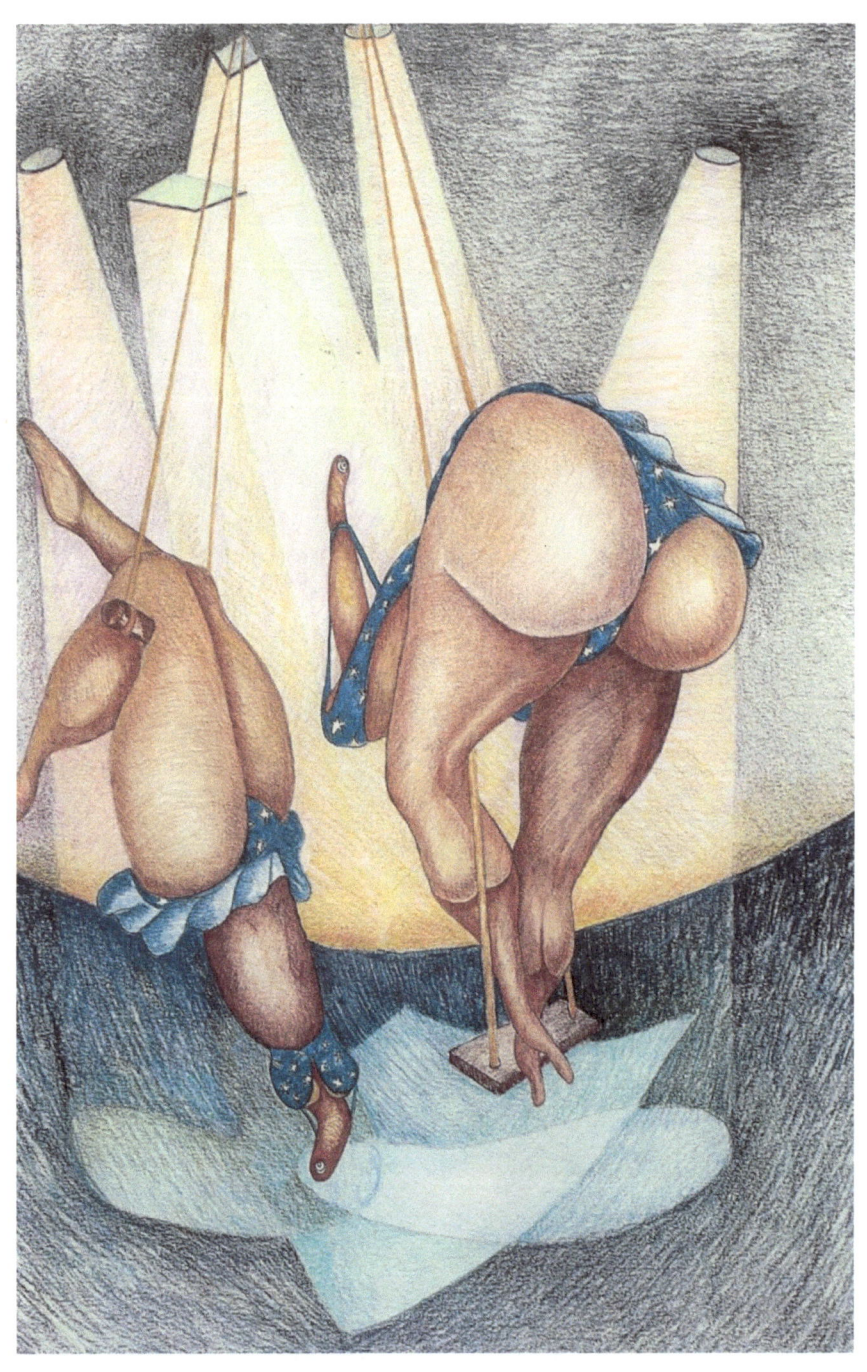

Molly Gwain-YA plays the "Hard to get Hard" teaser
To "Sneak-A-Peak" Polly Morph hanging upside-down
Hard winds below whip up the sea wall

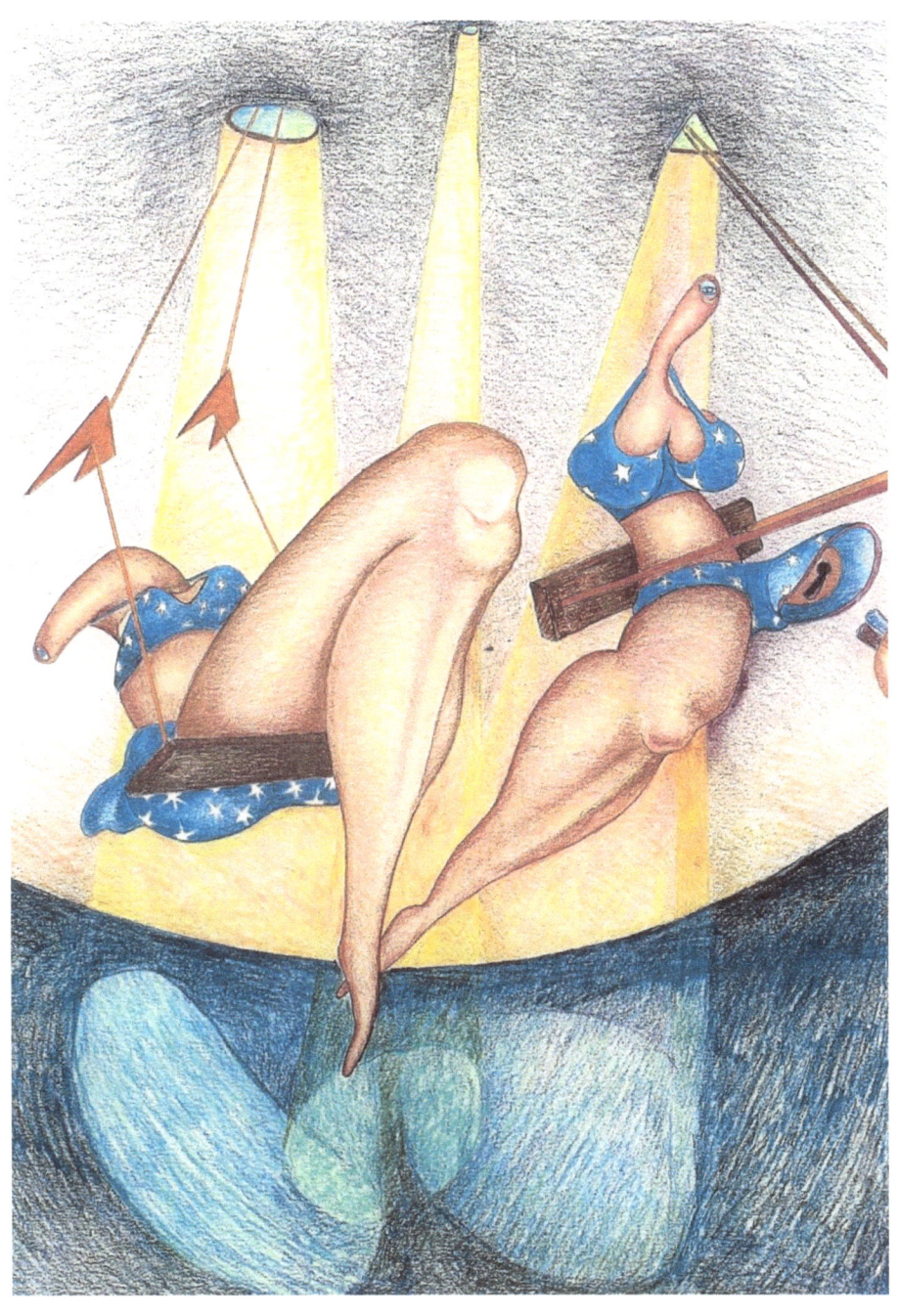

Molly Gwain-YA teases Polly Morph, until her legs fall off!
Time to get serious for this courtship of fools
Time is running out…Polly Morph drools!

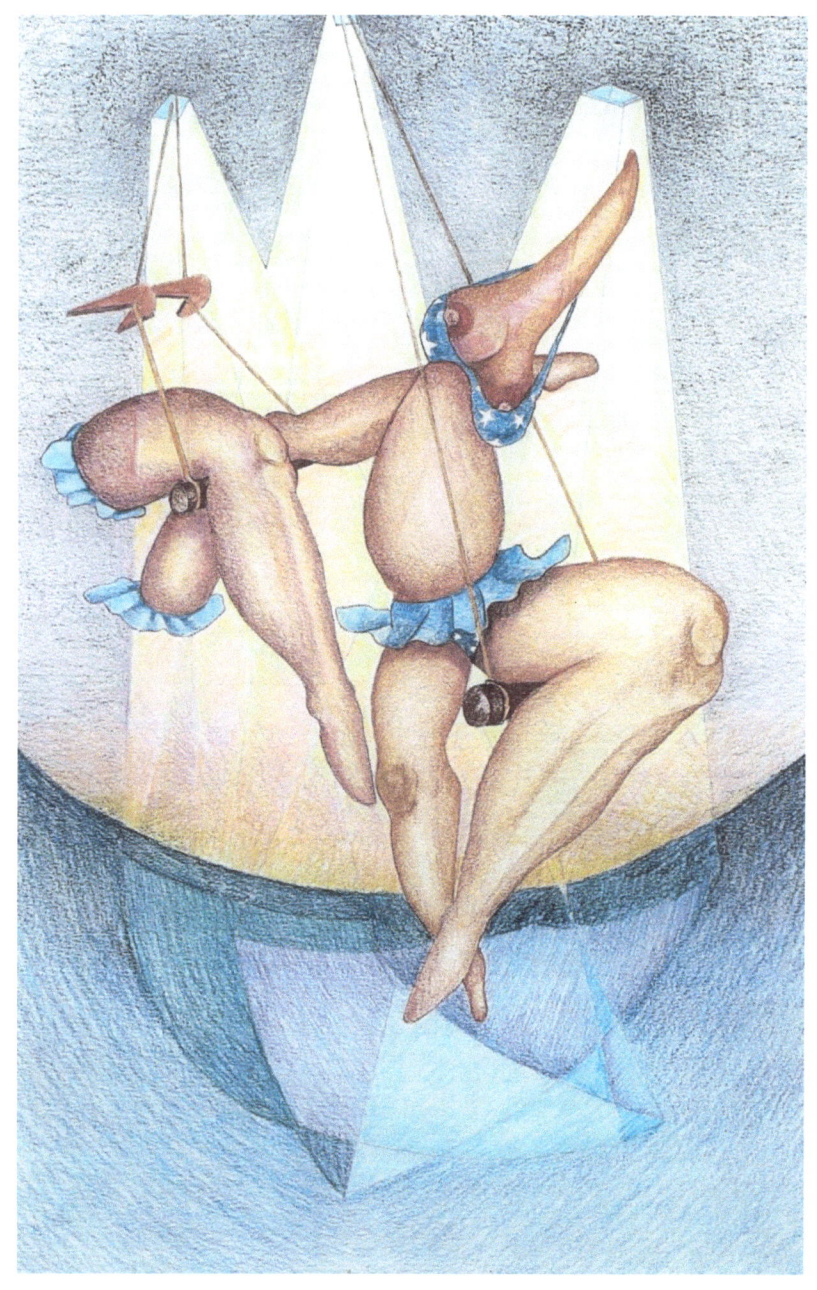

Polly Morph rescues both of Molly Gwain-YA's lost legs
And her "U know What" still intact will really please
Poor Molly Gwain-YA has lost her equilibrium and has
tumbled into the sea!

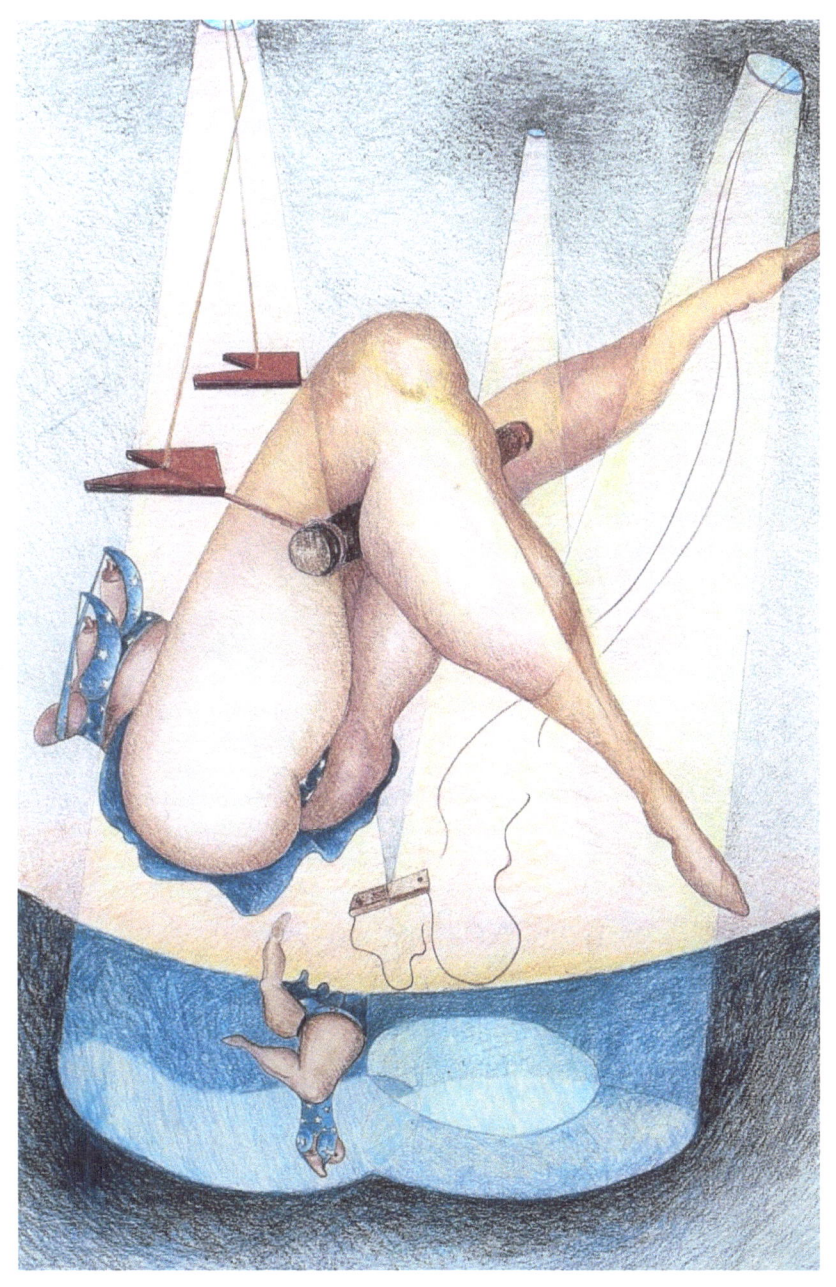

Molly Gwain-YA, the Anthropormorph, is humanly forsaken
On the way down to her watery grave.
Polly Morph turns a deaf ear
as Molly Gwain-YA is swept away

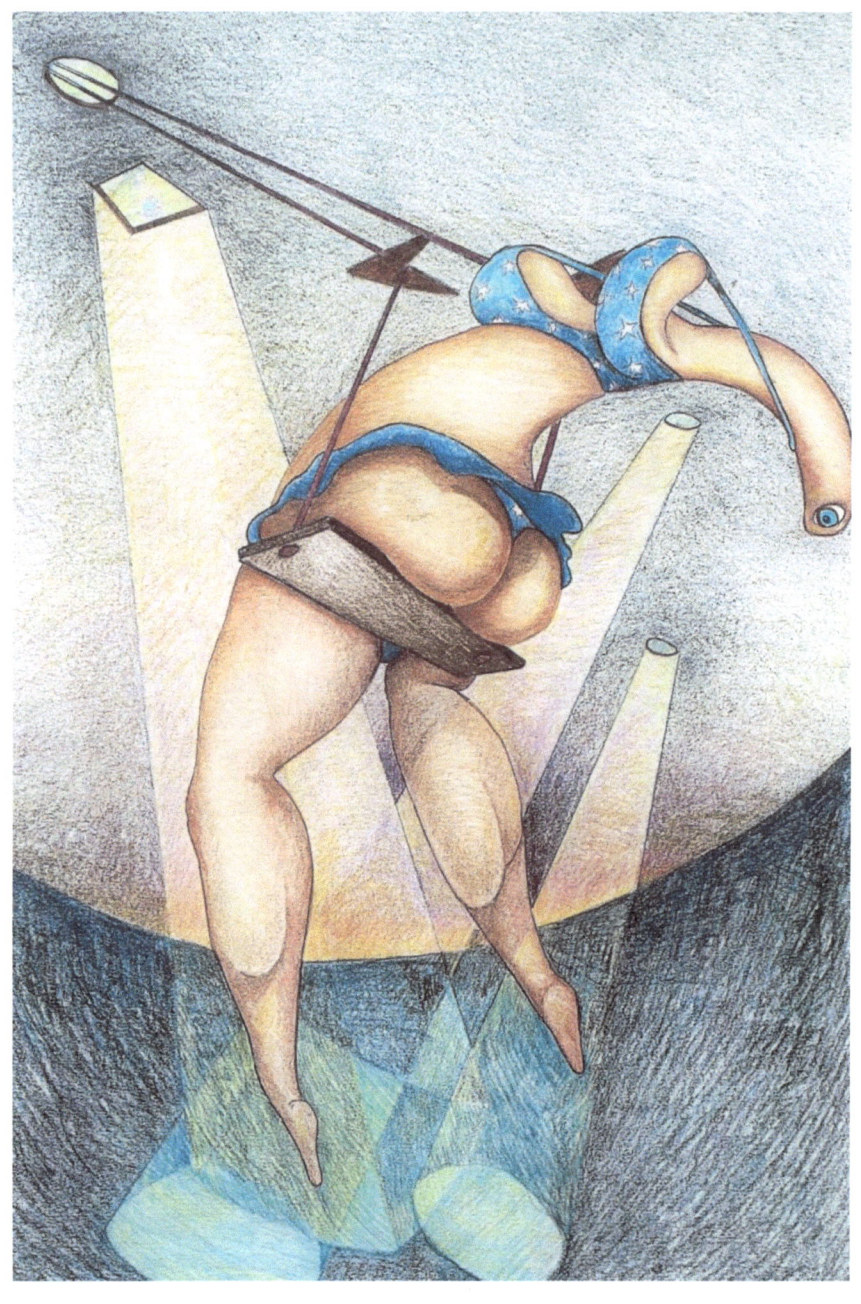

Polly Morph, that fickle Sea Ranger, pretends to search for her missing squeeze
Her treachery
Will soon be revealed, it has not gone unnoticed
Morph God smells a rat and Molly Gwain-YA is the cheese!

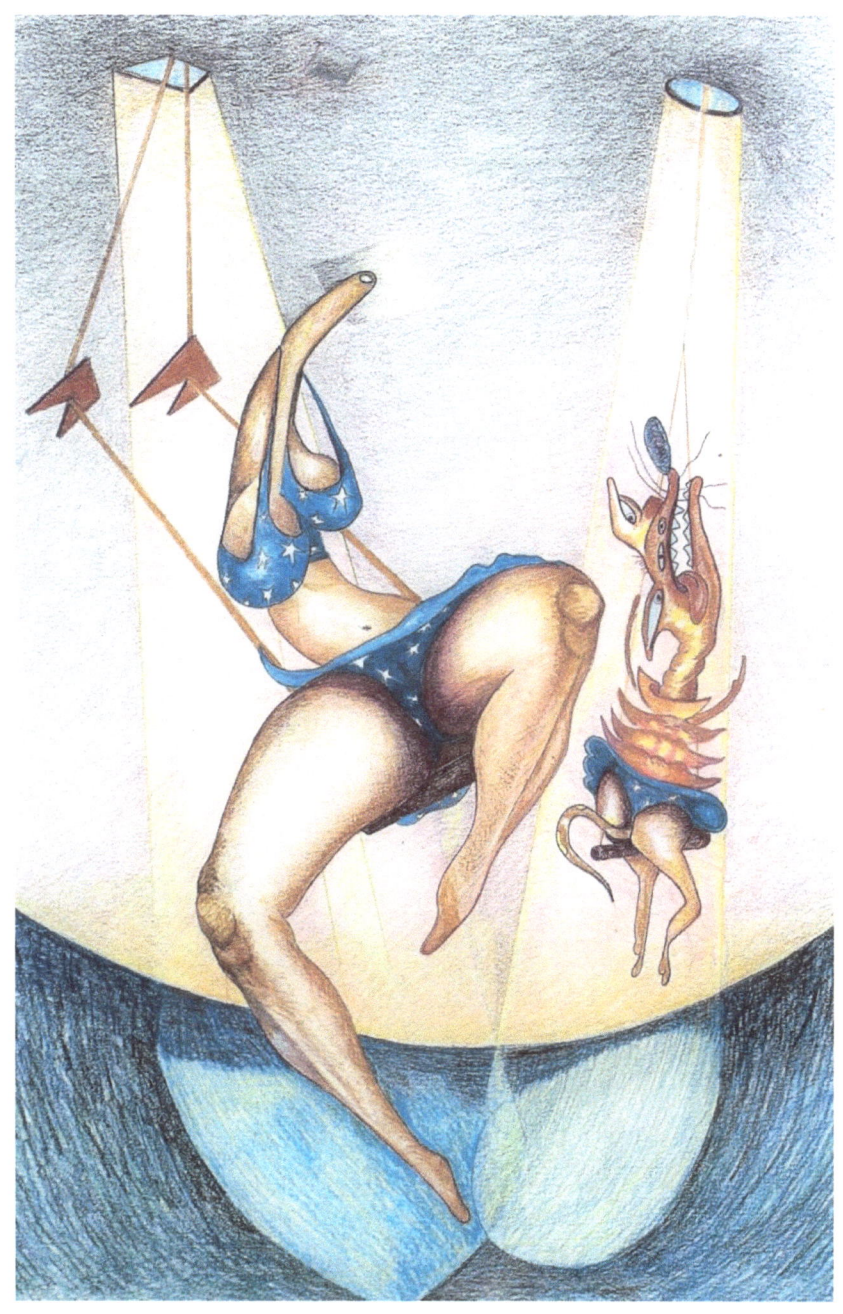

Molly Gwain-YA is resurrected in time for the Cirque de
Corporeal
Polly Morph is forever cursed and must obey
The trapeze tyrant: Dog Butt Ugly, from here to Eternity

Condemned to swing forever

with the Dog Butt Ugly show

The laughing stock

of the subterranean circus band

In the Cirque de Corporeal

with eccentric mutations

The Calamity of Desire

is more than she can stand

Letting go with no hands to begin with

No head to think

about "no more Head"

Anthropomorphous Polly

"forsaken, almost human"

Ends her life

in the Coliseum of despair

And desire, what is that?

You can ask me

If I tell you,

you will not want to know

The Anglopormorpho

tried to break it to you gently

But all you did was try to steal the show

Do not cry for the lost long liners

Don't curse where the Sea Rangers fail

Cry for the brave men of Gloucester

And the crew of the Andrea Gail

Raison d'Etre

by R.C. Webb

I began my study of painting and printmaking at East Carolina College in Greeneville, North Carolina, in the summer of '62. I had no interest in drawing or painting tobacco barns or other local color. Instead, I was drawn into the metaphysical paintings of deChirico, the critical paranoia of Dali, the visions of Tangy, and the automatisms of Miro, Klee, and Masson.

Intellectually, I was not involved with theory and made little sense of what Breton was telling the world about Surrealism. Being visually oriented, absorbing the power, form, and content of the painters--the Veristic wing of the Surrealist movement--came easily to me. I was seduced by those early mentors in the process of Surrealism, which became my life-long Raison d'Etre. My first Cause.

In 1970, I entered the so-called visionary cloisters of the San

Francisco Art Institute. California in the early seventies was a hotbed of political and artistic upheaval against the Vietnam War. With activist roots in the Civil Rights Movement and the Anti-War Movement, I was no stranger to these radical manifestations. The Visionary School, besides being archaic, boring, and irrelevant to current events soon collapsed in the exciting drama of street riots, inflammatory speeches, and guerilla art actions.

The School of Ultra-Realism emerged, and though not yet politicized, it drove the final stake into the heart of the tenured super heroes of Modernism. The New Radicalism in Art was on the march!

A new critical criteria for the advancement of Revolutionary Art theory was put forth, which, in essence stated that revolutionary art must have content which accurately represents the relationship between Victim, Enemy, and Solution, or V.E.S., in any given situation. It was discovered, in the course of training the propaganda wings of certain organizations, that lessons had to be created that did not require any artistic talent, per se, on the part of the group members. It was then discovered that, by cutting images out of Class-oriented magazines, such as *Better Homes and Gardens, Harpers Bazaar, Vogue,* etc. and putting them in a layout with images from the Black Book of Hunger, NACLA publications, and other radical sources, elements of syntax, such as tension, context, and proximity created intense psychological agitation. The addition of the Solution principal, depending on how violent or finite it was, was left to the particular group's philosophy and added the final touches to the work.

The V.E.S. principal soon had a following and evolved through dialogue, experimentation, and criticism into the School of Attack Surrealism. Although not a formal movement, more underground than not, kindred spirits were known, and not always to each other (for safety's sake), to be proliferating around the urban landscape from Los Angeles to Seattle, infiltrating and upstaging unworthy events, publishing violent manifestos, and most importantly, creating art in the V.E.S. genre.

The traditionally Surrealist technique of randomly combining seemingly obtuse visual elements to create a syntactical collapse to be replaced by a more powerful artistic idea served the propagandists well.

By not signing up for any particular "Solution," it was possible to avoid being sucked into ill-fated plots, all night arguments about content, and political correctness. The resulting works, built around Cezanne's Composition, were concise, forceful testimony both to our Movement and ourselves, and to the unhappy recipients of our ideas.

All through the remaining war years, and even into the 80s and 90s, I continued, almost in a vacuum to create hard-hitting, issue-oriented imagery (Anti-Nuke, AIDS, Religious Right, etc.) to continue illuminating the processes of my Surrealism.

My belief in the philosophical core of a socially virulent Surrealism has never waned. The politically caustic image in its Surrealist trappings or "The Surrealism in service to the Revolution" (a cult classic) had, for the most part, run its course.

The "Attack" principle, like the Phoenix, has risen from the ashes of the Left in a more psychological form, and the "Victim," as well as the "Enemy" are also back on line. The only difference between the old and the new is the context. For example, the original "Victim" was a socially recognized entity. Now, the "Victim" is the viewer, with all their hysterical dysfunction and sexual hang-ups. The "Enemy" is nothing less than the sum total of the Artist's own megalomaniacal need to divide and conquer the rational intrusions of the viewer into the destructive/creative cycle.

The "Solution" is entirely plausible as the view is confronted with the sardonic, sarcastic, and satirical non-factual truth of Veristicism; a politically challenged set of sexual assumptions; and a virtual, user-friendly alphabet of psych-iconography stewing in a post-psychotropic universe easily pilfered by the confused and vulnerable observer for their own perverse titillation or for self-indulgent pathos in a bloodless, non-violent context.

Attack Surrealism has put teeth back in the words of Breton and who-knows-what in the pantaloons of Dali. The important thing is that, as members in good standing or not, they have reached immortality together, sniggering like whores in a butt-rash clinic who, in spite of their incredible discomfort, know things could be a hell of a lot worse!

As for me, I will always push the Visionary envelope, as part of the New Surrealism or not, to bring the contradictions between our radical history and the egocentric reality of our artistic lives into some type of historical focus, both as artists/humans and citizens of the World.

You can follow me @burnt_lunch or visit my literary-artistic websites at www.blackcatpublishing.blogspot.com and www.burntlunch.blogspot.com.

See my artwork at www.imagekind.com; just search for "webbsurrealism" to see my galleries.